CW00385045

RISHTON REMEMBERED

by

Kathleen Broderick

Landy Publishing
1998

© Copyright in this book is held by
Kathleen Broderick and Landy Publishing.

ISBN 1 872895 42 5

British Library in Cataloguing Publication Data.
A catalogue record of this book is available from the British Library.

Layout by Mike Clarke, 01254 395848

Printed by Nayler the Printer Ltd., Accrington, 01254 234247

Landy Publishing have also published:

The Really Lancashire Book edited by Bob Dobson
Accrington Observed by Brian Brindle & Bob Dobson
Accrington's Changing Face by Frank Watson & Bob Dobson
An Accrington Mixture edited by Bob Dobson
Threads of Lancashire Life by Winnie Bridges
Lancashire, this, that an't'other by Doris Snape
Lancashire Laugh Lines by Kay Davenport
A Lancashire Look by Benita Moore
Blackburn in Times Gone By by Jim Halsall
The Blackburn Samaritan by Trevor Moore
A Blackburn Miscellany edited by Bob Dobson
Blackburn & Darwen A Century Ago by Alan Duckworth
Bits of Old Blackburn by Shaw & Hulme, illus. by Chas. Haworth
Blackburn's Shops at the Turn of the Century by Matthew Cole
Blackburn's West End by Matthew Cole

A full list is available from:

Landy Publishing
'Acorns' 3 Staining Rise, Staining, Blackpool, FY3 0BU
Tel/Fax: 01253 895678

INTRODUCTION

When I was fourteen, my grandmather Ormerod gave me a copy of *The Jubilee Souvenir of Rishton Parish Church & School*, which had been published ten years previously, in 1927. After reading the *History of Rishton* section by T. Carleton Noble, I was hooked. Ever since I have found the search for information on Rishton and its past wonderfully fascinating.

A rural village with small home-based industries of weaving and dying, Rishton changed little until 1851, when the first power-loom mill was built. The place became 'Boomtown'; a population of 800 in 1851 grew to 7,031 by 1901. House building began along the King's Highway and it became 'High Street', though locals called it 'Front Street'.

In a little over a hundred years, large scale textile production came and went, the last factory ceasing production in 1972. Even so, Rishton remains vibrant. The five settlements of Saxon times are still separate communities:- Holt, Rishton town, Tottleworth, Sidebeet and Cowhill.

I hope that this book revives memories for Rishtonians and gives an insight into Rishton's past to incomers of recent times.

Many people have helped in the compiling of this book by providing information or lending photographs. I specially want to thank Helen Barrett and Catherine Duckworth of the Accrington Local Studies Library who have patiently dealt with my numerous queries: Angela Hoyland of Rishton Library; and the staff at the County Record Office, especially Colin Duffield. I am greatly indebted to the elderly residents of Rishton, many of them no longer with us, for the information passed to me about the village in their young days. Lastly, I again mention T. Carleton Noble for igniting the first spark.

The book is based on the photographs made available to me by the following individuals, who deserve my thanks for their interest and kindness:- Mary Clark, nee Clarke, for permission to use the photos by the Counsells, her relatives, Doris Harrison, Edna Harrison, Marjorie Sharples, Elsie Smith, Irene Waddington, Bernard Bond, George Duckworth, Raymond Garrett, Roy Mackey, Allan Ormerod, Geoffrey Robinson, Gerald Rostron, David Sutcliffe, Donald Talbot and Jack Noble.

Kathleen Broderick.

Kathleen Broderick, nee Ormerod
August 1998

Front Cover: David Coleman and Thomas Robinson are seen in charge of 4 years old Walter Coleman and their van, Reg'd No. CB1, in 1919. Previously the vehicle's chassis had carried a charabanc. The High Street scene is described on page 24.

Thomas Counsell was a picture dealer who became a photographer. He had a shop and studio at 52, High Street. His son William carried on the business and was still in High Street in 1947. The shop appears in many photographs, as the tripod was set up on the high gardens across the road. Many of the photographs in this book were taken by Counsells. Without them this book would not be possible.

Holt was probably the earliest Saxon settlement in Rishton, and became the site of the medieval Manor House. A description of the hall as it was about 1540 says that it was moated, with a drawbridge and later a plain bridge. The Spaw Brook, which rises north of Blackburn Road, fed water to the moat. In the 18th century the Manor House had become a farmhouse, and was known as the Courthouse. The court met here twice a year to appoint a constable, a moorlooker and a pinder to catch stray animals. To the court came tenants complaining of neighbours who did not mend fences, scour ditches, who owed small amounts of money or would not return borrowed implements or ladders etc. In 1785 a second house had been erected in the fold, and on the site of this is the present farmhouse built about 1848.

Holt Mill, to every generation of Rishton people since Saxon times the mill driven by the River Hyndburn, would be a familiar sight. It stood on the south side of the road near the bridge, and the last traces were obliterated when the south side of the Paper Mill was built in 1904. Three storeys high with an overshot wheel, the mill ground oats, the staple diet of this area for centuries. Water was run off above the weir and stored in the mill pond. A sluice gate from the pond was opened when water was required to turn the mill wheel. Before oats could be ground they had to be dried in a kiln and until the early 17th century each hamlet had a kiln. There was one at Cowhill and one at Sidebeet. By the late 17th century all the oats were dried at the Holt kiln, which was north of the mill where the Paper Mill buildings now stand. All that remains of the mill workings is the weir, which in 1832 was 14 feet high. The miller's house stood west of the mill, but by 1826 the miller was the landlord of the Petre Arms, over the bridge in Clayton-le-Moors.

The Petre Arms, Clayton-le-Moors. There was probably an inn on this site long before, but the present building, with barn and cottages, is shown in 1785. Rishton tenants came here to pay their rents each year in May and November, and were provided with a dinner supplied by the innkeeper. The photograph appears to be taken about 1900. Since that time the road surface has risen considerably.

EACHILL FARM   A. Ormerod 1993

The name **Eachill** indicates land cleared and enclosed from the waste before 1100. The Whalley family were in Rishton before 1484 and were tenants of Eachill in 1599, still holding the lease until 1790 when Thomas Whalley died leaving the lease to his daughter Hannah Haworth.

This Tudor house had a double storey porch, which faced north, and mullioned windows splayed inside and out. In the main hall was the inglenook fireplace, common to the house of a yeoman farmer, and in the plasterwork opposite were the initials of James and Mary Whalley and the date 1678, indicating restoration at this time. There was a fine Jacobean staircase of two short flights with panels and spindles.

As the original entrance facing north was probably too draughty it was, at some time before the 20th century, blocked and a new entrance opened on the south side.

Rose Cottage, (*left*) Cowhill. This very sturdy cottage was one of the homes of the Hindle family, who bought land at Cowhill from Ralph Risheton of Dunkenhalgh in 1570. The Hindles were dealers and as early as 1569 sold linen cloth to Robert Nowell of the Read Hall family. The most notable member of the family was the Rev. Christopher Hindle, born 1592, who became vicar of Ribchester in 1617. During the Civil War he was not a '*staunch Royalist*' as previously believed, as he lent money to Parliament and paid the wages of a soldier. It was Christopher's opposition to the Presbyterian doctrine which got him into trouble with the church authorities. A believer in the Divine Right of Kings, from the pulpit he described the beheading of Charles I as '*that Scarlet Sin of Murder*'. Parliamentary soldiers who were present dragged him from the pulpit and threw him into the churchyard. He was deprived of his living and then returned to his cottage at Cowhill. The oak pulpit in Ribchester Church still bears his initials and the date 1636. His cottage, which now has dormer windows, is visible from the Blackburn to Accrington road near the Old Mother Redcap public house.

Parker's Farm or **Talbot's,** (*below*) Cowhill, got its present name from Christopher Parker, farmer, who was tenant in the early 19th century. It had a long history before that. Nikolaus Pevsner in his *Buildings of England* dates the house as early 17th century. Richard Talbot, who was granted a lease of the land in 1607, built the house. He was the grandson of Sir John Talbot od Salesbury and Sir Richard Hoghton of Lea. He was bailiff to Judge Walmsley, and would oversee his master's land and property in Rishton, wearing his blue coat, supplied periodically. The tenement remained in his family until 1804. The house that Richard built, though now disused, is a listed building for its architectural and historical interest. The central chimney served two back-to-back fireplaces, one the inglenook in the hall or living room, and one the service room, sometimes used for agricultural rather than domestic purposes, which sometime before 1915 was opened at the front and used as a cartshed. At the west end, with the external chimney, were a small parlour and behind it a pantry. English Heritage have included Parker's Farm, a Grade II listed building, amongst their *Buildings at Risk*.

Master Barn Farm, (*below*). Rishton Tithe Barn stood here. The barn with 30 acres of arable land, 13 acres of meadow, 20 acres of pasture and 2 acres of woodland, was sold by Ralph Rishton to Judge Thomas Walmesley in 1601 for £40. A house was erected in 1675 and is now incorporated into agricultural buildings. In 1680 it was agreed by the Jury of the Manor Court that the Tithe Barn and outhousing should be let.

The circular track in the yard of Master Barn Farm was used by a donkey, which walked round and turned a butter churn. It must have been constructed in the 19th century, as it is on the line of the turnpike road which was diverted in 1826. Henry Petre in 1861 erected the present farmhouse, then known as East White House.

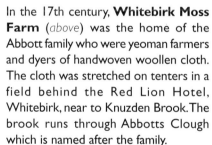

In the 17th century, **Whitebirk Moss Farm** (*above*) was the home of the Abbott family who were yeoman farmers and dyers of handwoven woollen cloth. The cloth was stretched on tenters in a field behind the Red Lion Hotel, Whitebirk, near to Knuzden Brook. The brook runs through Abbotts Clough which is named after the family.

During the Civil War looters stole £6 in gold, three silver spoons worth 7s 6d and clothes worth £1 10s from Grace Abbott of Whitebirk. In the middle of the 17th century, though occupied by the Abbotts, the lease was held for a time by Thomas Whalley of Blackburn, known as *Duke of the Bank*, after whom Duke's Brow was named. Whitebirk was for many years after known as Duke House. In 1675 the house was renovated and reroofed with slates from Green Haworth, Accrington.

The area known as **New Inns** on the old road from Rishton to Preston, via Ribchester, gets its name from the 'New Inn'. The earliest known mention of the New Inn is on 6th June, 1624, when John Hindle of the New Inn, Rishton, was buried at Blackburn. The original inn was a small cottage on the side of the road from Rishton, but between 1785 and 1818 the licence was moved to a farmhouse across the road.

Near the New Inn the road is joined by roads from Little Harwood and Great Harwood. In the 18th and early 19th centuries drovers from Scotland passed on their way to sell beasts at Great Harwood Fair, held annually on 21st August.

Sir James Kay Shuttleworth describing his memories of about 1814 writes: "*The young

stock fed during the summer on the moorland pastures were driven from the fells of Shap and Westmorland... Scotch bonnet and maud (a woollen plaid), and the tartan scarf and trews of the half-savage lads who, with bare feet and legs, and armed with long hazel sticks, helped the dogs to keep the flocks together. Strings of unkempt ponies, with shaggy manes and long tails, and herds of longhorn cattle, Ayrshire milking stock, and the small Westmorland black-faced sheep crowded the narrow lanes.*"

By 1854 the New Inn had been renamed The Bay Horse, but local people still used the old name.

Norden Farm. The common was enclosed in 1786 and Norden was leased to Thomas Bulcock, Gent. of Micklehey. He was to erect at his own proper cost, charge and expense a good, substantial and sufficient new stone Dwelling House and one Barn including Shipponing for 16 cows and a Stable for 5 horses, finding slate, stone to finish and complete the same.

The photograph shows Norden Farm in 1974. Notice the classical doorframe.

CLOSE BROW
RISHTON.

Close Brow, above circa 1910, and left in the 1950s. Close Nook Farm and Star Delph, halfway up the hill, are on the right in the second photograph. The cyclist would have to get off and push. The prominent line of trees along the ridge, which is visible for miles and is described on ordnance maps as '*Top o' th' Heights*', was planted in 1819. Many of the trees were dead in 1953 and new trees were planted as part of the Coronation celebrations.

Close Nook. The land north of Lee Lane was enclosed in 1666 and became known as New Close. A lease dated 13th June, 1752, was given to John Duxbury *'on consideration of erecting a dwelling-house of two bays and a barn of two bays at the corner of New Close'*. The date on the lintel of the house is 1755.

Occupied by members of the family of George Clarke during the late 19th century, it became known as Clark's Farm. Acquired by Lancashire County Council in 1909, the property was sold in 1979 and the barn was converted into a second dwelling.

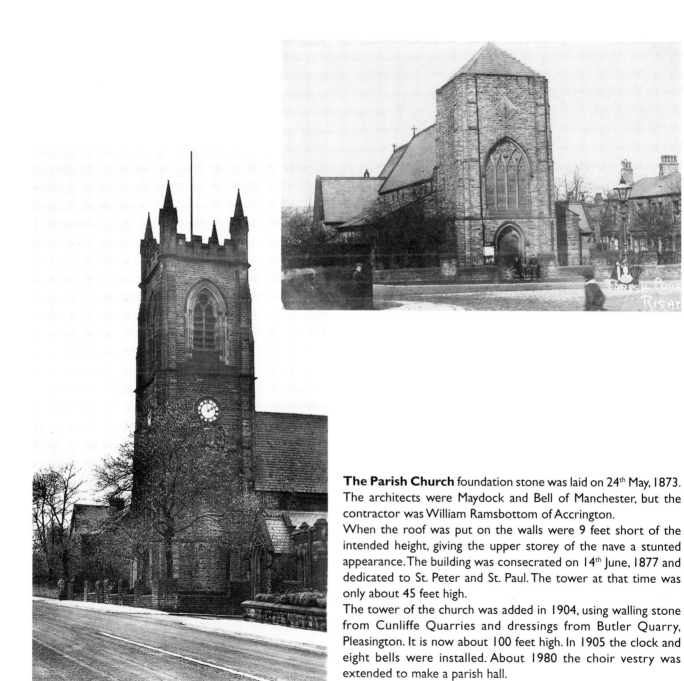

The Parish Church foundation stone was laid on 24th May, 1873. The architects were Maydock and Bell of Manchester, but the contractor was William Ramsbottom of Accrington.

When the roof was put on the walls were 9 feet short of the intended height, giving the upper storey of the nave a stunted appearance. The building was consecrated on 14th June, 1877 and dedicated to St. Peter and St. Paul. The tower at that time was only about 45 feet high.

The tower of the church was added in 1904, using walling stone from Cunliffe Quarries and dressings from Butler Quarry, Pleasington. It is now about 100 feet high. In 1905 the clock and eight bells were installed. About 1980 the choir vestry was extended to make a parish hall.

13

Before the 1939-45 war, every Whit weekend saw half the village praying for dry weather. On Monday morning out came crowds of children, with girls in new dresses, some with baskets or crooks trimmed with flowers - lillies were the first choice. The flowers were bought on Saturday and kept in buckets of water in the coolest place to be found. All church organisations took part in the procession, which started from the school in Harwood Road and stopped outside the Church to sing the first hymn. It then moved by stages to St. Andrew's Mission, singing more hymns at various halts. By lunch time the procession was over, but the best was yet to come. A kind farmer provided a field, often in Stourton Street where Norden School now stands. Carts with trays of large currant buns and urns of coffee drew crowds of children.

This burlesque Cricket Team took part in the Diamond Jubilee celebrations of the Church. Judging by the size of the bat and balls it must have been a great match. In the photograph from the left are: Billy Cottham, Billy Schaeffer, ...?, ...?, Tom Watson, Jim Clarke, Riley Duckworth, Rev. Ira Brown, Tom Porter, Jimmy Haslam. In front are: Billy Dawson, Dick Wilkinson, Jack Slater, John Duckworth.

BURLESQUE CRICKET TEAM

RISHTON PARISH CHURCH DIAMOND JUBILEE CELEBRATIONS JUNE 16TH 1937

"OLD FOLKS' TREAT."

Rishton, Feb. 18th, 1899.

Dear Sir or Madam,

The Contributors to the Fund for providing the above request the pleasure of your Company to * * *

High Tea, Concert and Social,

On Wednesday, February 22nd, 1899.

JOS. MARSHALL,
Chairman.

J. J. ADAMS,
Secretary.

To Mr and Mrs. Walton.

20. 21.

The Post Office at 9, High Street, is mentioned in 1868. The cotton millowners placed a clock in the window in 1875, and from the time shown by this clock, late-comers at the local mills were fined.

In the doorway are two daughters of John Taylor, the Postmaster. He had previously been Station Master at Rishton. By 1909 the Post Office had moved to its present position at 13, High Street. This photograph was taken in the 1890s.

Born in Grandborough, Buckinghamshire, a brickmaking area, George Clarke worked on railway construction in Derbyshire and Gloucestershire. He was appointed in 1848 to make the seven million bricks needed to build the Whalley Viaduct. On his thirty-second birthday in 1851 he moved to Rishton, and following him came a number of families, many of them relatives, from Buckinghamshire and neighbouring counties. There were Colemans, Quaintons, Bedfords and Richardsons, and by 1871 they constituted four percent of the population of Rishton. This photo from the Clarke family album shows George with his son Mark and Mark's wife.

GEORGE CLARKE,
RISHTON,
NEAR BLACKBURN, LANCASHIRE,
MANUFACTURER OF
CRUCIBLES, CLAY RETORTS,
SANITARY TUBES,
FIRE BRICKS,
COMMON BRICKS, DRAINING TILES, CHIMNEY TOPS, &c., &c.

The Bricks are used commonly instead of the Leeds and Stourbridge Bricks in many furnaces and give general satisfaction.

One Gentleman says of them : " They stand the heat better than any we have tried, and we shall continue to use them."

An Agent of a Gas Company also says : " Your best Fire Bricks stand better than any we have tried from this neighbourhood, and you may forward us 1,500 more of them, as we shall use them for high heats."

Messrs. William Blythe and Co. observe : " We have found your best Fire Bricks very good for all purposes, as good as any we have tried. We wish you to send us 3,000 of your best some time this week."

Mr. Joseph Barnes says : " I can safely recommend your Fire Bricks for Coke Ovens ; ours have been in regular work above four years, and have not a single complaint. The ovens I built in March, 1853, are in excellent order, and I do not hear of a bad brick in the whole of fifty ovens."

The Works are by the Canal ; Bricks can be sent by Boat or by Rail from the Rishton Station, to any place where purchasers require them. All shapes made to order.

ALSO QUARRYMASTER IN
FLAGS, SIDESTONES, LONG STONE COVERS,
LANDINGS, DOOR CHEEKS, WINDOW BOTTOMS, PARPOINTS, CHANNEL STONES, SETTS, &c., &c.
CUNLIFFE QUARRY ROCK & GREET ROCK.

George lived in Mary Street, but by 1861 had moved to Norden View, and was a brickmaker and quarrymaster, employing 30 men and boys. He used shale from Close Brow quarry and from Rishton Pit, and much of it was suitable for making fire bricks used to build coke ovens, furnaces and fire backs. The works closed in 1960. George was instrumental in the building of Victoria Mill, the largest in Rishton. Hearing of six businessmen in Bacup who intended to build a mill, George Clarke joined them and was able to persuade them to come to Rishton. The mill built in 1861-3 was long known as the 'Bacup Co-op'. He died in 1909 aged 90, having made a great impression on the village, both industrially and through his work in establishing the Wesleyan Chapel.

R. BUTLER & SON LTD.
JOINERS
Funeral Directors
Spring Street Saw Mills, Rishton
Telephone : Gt. Harwood 2142

Wesleyan Procession in Cliff Street, 1929. The railings surrounded the Council Yard where road mending equipment and paving stones were kept. The sweetshop, where the possessor of a halfpenny could buy *fat ducks, green peas and new potatoes*', belonged to Miss Hollinrake

RISHTON
WESLEYAN
Sunday-School Sermons.

You are respectfully informed that on Sunday,
August 4th, 1861,

TWO SERMONS
WILL BE PREACHED IN
MR. GEORGE CLARKE'S BRICK SHED,
(*In consequence of the present Preaching Room being too small,*)

By Mr. E. Nuttall,
OF BOLTON,
When Collections will be made in behalf of the intended New School.

Service to commence in the Afternoon at half-past Two o'clock, and in the Evening at Six.

IN THE MORNING AT HALF-PAST TEN,
AN ADDRESS WILL BE DELIVERED
BY
MR. WILLIAM WORKMAN,
OF RISHTON,
To Parents, Teachers, Scholars, and Friends.

Your attendance on the occasion is earnestly solicited.

PRINTED FOR MRS. ELL'SON, OAKENSHAW.

18

Wesleyan Chapel, Rishton.

An early band of Wesleyans, six in 1809, and a different six some twenty years later, had ceased to exist by 1831. Another group started in 1836, but survived for only four years. They held their meetings in the cottage of Henry Noble in High Street, which was one of the buildings where the Clinic and Bank later stood. When George Clarke came to Rishton with his relatives in 1851, he held meetings for Wesleyans in his house No. 2, Mary Street. Two upper rooms of 138, High Street, which belonged to Mr. Clarke, were made into one and a Sunday School commenced. When two upper rooms of an adjoining cottage were added, about two hundred people could be seated.

The Society flourished and in 1861 a special service was held in Mr. Clarke's brick shed. George wished to build a chapel and secured land in High Street, from the canal to Henry Street, but the Wesleyan circuit authorities would not agree and cut the area to half. The chapel was built in 1862 and later enlarged, a school was built and a gallery installed in the chapel. In 1897, *Sunnybank* in Blackburn Road, now a private residential home, was built for the use of the minister.
On Saturday 25th August, 1973, a new Methodist Church was opened, and the old chape was converted into flats.

Hermitage Street. The turnpike road was diverted in 1826 to relieve the hill, then called Holt Mill Brow, to form a regularly inclined plane from a new bridge intended to be erected over the River Hyndburn at Holt Mill to the Canal Bridge, thus forming the present line of Hermitage Street. The street takes its name from the school erected in 1819. The row of bay-windowed houses, on the right of the view, was known as '*key row*'. Each front door had a large knob in the centre which served little purpose. To enter the house it was necessary to unlock the door with the key.

The Hermitage, Rishton's first known school, near the site of West White House, High Street, close to the junction with Harwood Road, was run by John Simpson, who in 1804 had about 20 pupils. In 1819 George Petre, Lord of the Manor, built its successor and the name Hermitage was transferred. By the 1830s the school seems to have closed and the property was let to three tenants. In 1851 Richard Bilsborough a tenant there who was a calico printer, taught pupils, probably on Sundays. The Hermitage is now a private residence.

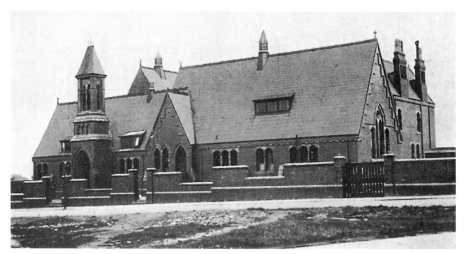

In 1886 a **Roman Catholic Mission** was started at the Hermitage, and a building at the rear which had been the joiner's shop of James Knowles became a Roman Catholic School. When the Roman Catholics opened their new school in Knowles Street in 1896 the Church of England aquired the old joiner's shop, and in May 1897 opened St.Andrew's Mission there.The Catholic School in Knowles Street had the name Hermitage St. Charles, but as this was confusing it was dropped in 1957 and the sole name St. Charles was used.The church was built in 1938.

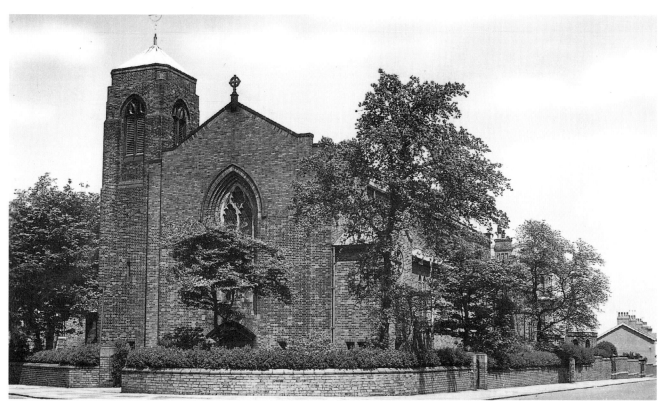

The Primitive Methodists started a Society holding meetings in the cottage of John Holding in Tottleworth. The little congregation increased so the Primitives built a barn-like chapel where Knowles Street now meets Clarke Street. After seven years this was 'crowded out' and a new school/chapel was erected in School Street. The corner stone was laid on 2nd October 1875 and the building first used on 15th July 1876. In the late 1880s the Day School children and master of the Methodist Free Church in Mary Street joined the Primitives. It was necessary to extend the School Street premises in 1910, and £1,000 was needed, but how to raise it? A Bazaar and a borrowed barrel-organ. The Day School closed in 1943.

The photograph was taken near the Post Office at No. 13. It is probably a Saturday afternoon with little traffic in 1911. Notice the setts in the road.

The Funeral of Fr. James Higgins, who had become Rector of St. Charles' R. C. Church in 1903. He extended the church considerably and his Silver Jubilee was celebrated in 1922. He died suddenly on Tuesday 28th October, 1924, aged 51, and had established himself firmly in the affections of his parishioners.

Requiem Mass was celebrated on Friday 31st October, and a choir of priests from all over the country sang parts of the service. There were 63 priests present.

Fr. Higgins was interred at St. Hubert's and the route from Rishton to Great Harwood was lined by crowds of people. There were 350 people in the procession, including all the church organisations.

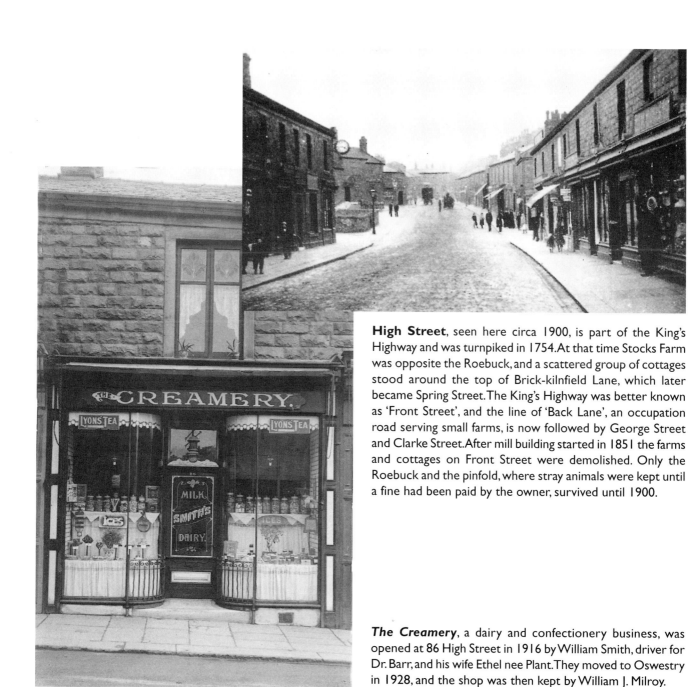

High Street, seen here circa 1900, is part of the King's Highway and was turnpiked in 1754. At that time Stocks Farm was opposite the Roebuck, and a scattered group of cottages stood around the top of Brick-kilnfield Lane, which later became Spring Street. The King's Highway was better known as 'Front Street', and the line of 'Back Lane', an occupation road serving small farms, is now followed by George Street and Clarke Street. After mill building started in 1851 the farms and cottages on Front Street were demolished. Only the Roebuck and the pinfold, where stray animals were kept until a fine had been paid by the owner, survived until 1900.

The Creamery, a dairy and confectionery business, was opened at 86 High Street in 1916 by William Smith, driver for Dr. Barr, and his wife Ethel nee Plant. They moved to Oswestry in 1928, and the shop was then kept by William J. Milroy.

RISHTON FROM THE TOWER.

High Street from the Church Tower. On the north side of High Street were three old cottages, 108, 110 and 112 High Street, which had been made from very old farm buildings. In 1899 the Council described them as '*dangerous, injurious to health and unfit for human habitation*', giving the owner Henry Petre seven days to improve them. He must have declined as the cottages disappeared. One elderly resident remembered the tenants as *Old Cowell*, who sold hot peas from his cottage every night, *Pickled Onion Jane* and *the Limping Clogger*. The cottages must have been low as another elderly gentleman admitted that, as boys, he and his friends would climb up and put sods on the chimneys.

The photograph in 1905 shows an empty space. Shortly after, John Parker, architect, built a house, later the Clinic, and in 1909 the bank, now a restaurant, was erected.

High Street, Harwood Road Corner at ten minutes past eleven on a quiet morning in the late 1920s. George Monk, Tripe Dresser, owned several shops in the Blackburn area. Tripe was delivered to Rishton shops by horse and cart.

The bus shelter and public conveniences at Harwood Road corner were built in 1924. The shelter became known as the '*Cold Feet Club*', as it became the daily meeting-place of the elderly gentlemen of the village, where great deliberations took place and the world was set to rights.

HIGH ST. RISHTON.

Lee Lane, the road from Rishton to Great Harwood, was a track across the common. Even after the opening of the Leeds & Liverpool Canal and the building of Norden Bridge in 1810, it was only cartwidth. In 1894 a deep depression at Norden was filled but Lee Lane was still only a narrow thoroughfare with no footpath. In the 1930s Capt. C. B. Petre gave land for a road widening scheme. Bends were eliminated as far as possible, the gradient improved and footpaths constructed. Work commenced in May 1936, and on 3rd August, 1938 John Booth, Chairman of the Buildings and Highways Committee performed the opening ceremony by cutting a red, white and blue tape.

Along Lee Lane during the Second World war were containers of heavy oil. On moonlit nights the oil was burned producing evil-smelling smoke, which blanketed the area to make it difficult for enemy aircraft to pinpoint the Bristol Aircraft Factory at Clayton-le-Moors and impossible for local people to leave windows open.

The Esplanade. On the same day, after the ceremony at Lee Lane, land given by Capt. Petre, to be an open space for all time, was dedicated to the inhabitants of Rishton by Councillor Booth. The Surveyor, Mr. W. H. Renshaw, planned the area, which was almost an acre in extent, with a frontage of 668 feet. Five circular beds of roses and lawns with herbaceous borders were constructed, around which were asphalted paths. The development took a year and cost about £1.000.

VIEW IN CUTT WOOD PARK. RISHTON.

COUNSELL. RISHTON.

The name of **Cutt or Cutte Park** is derived from Cuttleleach Meadows, two fields situated down what has become known as Cutte Lane. During the 18th century the fields were leased to the tenant of Cuttleleach Farm on the south side of Cowhill. In the 1930s Cutte Wood in Spring was full of bluebells. The land was given by Capt. C. B. Petre and was laid out as a park. On the 29th August, 1936 it was dedicated by Mr. T. C. Bracewell, J. P., C. C. of Ingleneuk, Station Road, who opened the ornamental gates which he had presented.

In the photograph of the opening are, from the left: the Rev. Ira Brown, Miss Priscilla Bracewell, Councillor Thomas Porter, Mr. T. W. Bracewell, Councillors Alfred Trengrove, John W. Booth, Mr. W. R. Renshaw, Surveyor who planned the park, Councillors Herbert Wilson and Benjamin Ainsworth (cinema owner).

BLACKBURN RD. FROM TOWER RISHTON.

Blackburn Road in 1904. Next to the Church is the Vicarage built in 1880, then Moor House erected by Edward Eccles, owner of Wheatfield Mill, in 1886. The third house, The Turrets, was the home of Robert Clayton, one of the partners of Bridgefield Mill, also built in 1886. Highfield Road was not yet built, but the Cricket Field is visible. Millworkers played cricket at lunchtime in the yard of the Victoria or 'Co-op' mill, and then received permission to play in the adjoining field. In 1865 the club was formed and played on a rented field on the south side of the railway station, now part of the golf course. The panelled brick wall in Blackburn Road was erected about 1930.

Station Road, Rishton

Station Road, prior to 1885, was a rough roadway, only 18 feet wide with no footpath, leading to the station. In that year the Railway Company widened the road by three feet on the west and constructed a six foot footpath on the east. The road was then taken over by the Local Board. When houses were erected in Station Road the width was extended to 27 feet with footpaths nine feet wide. Mr. Thomas Seed donated a lamp-post near to the church as a guide for returning travellers on dark nights.

The Roebuck was both farm and inn. The lower part with cottage and barn is old, as the upper mullioned window suggests 17th century, and being the centre of 'Rishton Town' it is likely that there was an inn there in medieval times. The inn was extended in 1753, in anticipation of coaching trade, as the road was to be turnpiked the following year. The datestone bears the initials of Thomas and Grace Duckworth, who were there in 1750 and whose family held the tenancy for three generations, their lease ending in 1842. In 1785 the Manor Court was meeting there twice a year '*at the house of Joseph Duckworth*', and he supplied dinners to the jury of fifteen tenants. The inn was called The Stag, but the name was changed to Roebuck in 1854.

The Roebuck was sold by auction for £22,600 in December 1897 to Messrs. Cunningham and T. & W. Thwaites of Blackburn. In 1898 they submitted plans for alterations, probably the removal of the Georgian windows and the addition of the shell-hood.

The barn was demolished about 1920, but the setts still show the road to the barn door. Animals straying on to the common were put into the pinfold or pound and kept until the owner paid a fine.

In the top photograph of circa 1890 the youths are standing by the wall of the pinfold, then being used for storage purposes. Again the site is visible by the layout of the setts.

A delivery to the **Roebuck** circa 1910. The Billiard Hall, first licensed in 1914, has not yet appeared. The lorry is an early Leyland Motors product, first registered in Preston. Matthew Brown & Co. brewed their 'Lion' beer in Blackburn until the 1980s when the Scottish & Newcastle brewery company closed down the brewery but kept the trading name.

Telephone : GREAT HARWOOD 2202

WEST END GARAGE

(W. CURREN, *Proprietor*)

MOTOR ENGINEER :: RISHTON

Tyres, Oils, Petrol, Spares, etc.
Complete Car Overhauls, Rebores, etc.
Taxis available for all Occasions.

The Conservative Working Men's Club was formed in 1873. A cottage on Petre Row, number 52, High Street was rented, and soon after a three-storey club was erected at 61, High Street. The formal opening was on 30th November, 1878, but the club had then been in use for almost a year. The ground floor housed two shops and the club keeper's residence. A large newsroom and two small card or draughts rooms occupied the first floor, and the second contained two billiard tables. The foundation stone of the present club on Cliff Street was laid on 12th November, 1896, and it was opened on 16th June, 1900.

J. & H. Smith, Printers, moved into 61, High Street. In the photograph Henry Smith is standing in the doorway and a placard reads 'Russian Grand Duke Blown to Pieces' which indicates that the photo was taken soon after the 28th June 1914, when the assasination which lead to the First World War occurred.

Telephone: 3289 GREAT HARWORD

WORTH-MOR MEATS

Proprietor: W. HAWORTH

Specialists in Beef and Salmon Paste

COOKED MEATS OF QUALITY

◇

WORTH-MOR BUILDINGS,
SPRING STREET, RISHTON

Festival of Britain, 1951. 'Our Glorious Empire' - rather late! The Women's Unionist float in Clifton Street outside the Conservative Club.

The Rishton Arms, near to the station, was completed and a licence granted to Daniel Thwaites in 1878. The bowling green fell into disuse after the Second World War.

The Coronation of King George VI, 1937. Flags were everywhere. Bunting was strung across streets, many of which had parties for the children. The party in the photograph was in Fielding Street. There was a procession, followed in the afternoon by races and a coffee and bun. Every child was measured in school and was presented with a blazer, a medal and a mug. This was a repetition of the Jubilee celebration of King George V in 1935. The blazers were dark blue with red, white and blue piping. They were very welcome as many parents were unemployed or '*playing for beams*', which meant working all week with one or even two of the weaver's looms standing idle.

RELIABILITY is the keynote of

GEORGE HARWOOD & SON

N.A.F.D.

JOINERS · BUILDERS · CONTRACTORS

Jobbing Work a Speciality

COMPLETE FUNERAL DIRECTORS

◇

Works and Saw Mills:

CANAL YARD, End of Spring Mill

Residence:

69, SPRING STREET, RISHTON

Cremations, Embalmers, etc.

Funerals carried out with economy and refinement. Personal Supervision

The Coronation, 1953. York Mill yard, with the portrait of the Queen which later hung in the canteen for some years. Below is the bench of tackler Richard Livesey, decorated for the occasion.

Coleman and Robinson. William Coleman of 6, Mary Street, was a descendant of a Buckinghamshire family. In 1897 he was a coal dealer and haulier. After his death his wife Mary, who gave her name to the street, carried on the business. Their horses, seen below and which appear on the front cover, were stabled in Noble Street. They later acquired motorised vehicles. The charabanc B5725 of 1903 is taking a party of Wesleyans on an outing shortly before 1914.

The charabanc outside the Parish Church, with Thomas Robinson still in uniform, was first registered by G. H. Woods of Blackburn, and later purchased by Coleman and Robinson. This Alldays vehicle CB1 was not very reliable, and was said to be 'Allday in use and allnight under repair'.

One of Coleman and Robinson's lorries was used by the army to haul supplies during the 1914-18 war. Thomas Robinson accompanied the vehicle as driver.

Reservoir House. In 1785 there was a small enclosure called Aincross on Rishton Moor, with a house, a meadow and a pasture. Near this small farm of only nine acres, two streams ran from Cowhill and crossed the rough track over the moor which the present Blackburn Road follows. The streams fed the canal reservoir when it was built in 1828, and about that time the house was renovated or rebuilt. Due to sand quarrying in the area in the 19th century the house became known as Sandholes. In 1909 it was occupied by John Plant, a descendant of a Buckinghamshire family, and in 1928 George Plant started a business there as wheelwright and motor body builder. By 1939 the house was known as Reservoir House, and in the 1980s it was demolished.

Mr G Plant

A businessman who founded a Rishton firm and helped run it for more than half a century died last Saturday.

He was 78-year-old Mr George Plant, who started his own business, Plants Motor Bodies, in Blackburn-road in 1928 and stayed closely involved in the firm until it was sold to Warwick and Bailey a year ago.

Mr Plant of Whalley-road, Wilpshire, died in Withington Hospital, Manchester, after undergoing a major operation.

His wife Elizabeth died in February this year and their son Ronald, who had helped in the business, died two years ago at the age of 52.

Barnston. John Parker, architect, who built and lived at 110 High Street, left Rishton and lived in Canada for a time. On his return he built Barnston in Blackburn Road, near to the reservoir. It was later owned by the Smith family. In 1976 it was sold and was demolished soon after. The owner of the bungalow enjoyed boating rights on the reservoir.

In 1828, **The Reservoir** was constructed to store water to supply the Leeds & Liverpool Canal when required. It is fed by two streams which flow from Cowhill. The East Lancashire Railway, opened in 1848, crossed the reservoir by means of a timber viaduct, with 18 openings each 12 feet wide.

The reservoir was also used for recreation. On Sunday 30th January, 1870, there were hundreds of skaters. The ice cracked and nine skaters, holding hands in a line, were plunged into the water. Helpers used tree branches, coats, a ladder and reins to rescue five, but three women drowned. The inquest was held at the Walmesley Arms on the following Tuesday.

Between Easter Monday and the 10th May, 1890, three hundred Loch Leven trout over eight inches in length were landed. One angler caught 38 in one day.

'*Have you heard the Rishton nightingale?*' In June 1893 thousands came in one week alone to the wood near the reservoir, and '*listened in rapt attention*' between 9.0pm and 3.0am though many had to go to work early next morning. On Saturday £6-18s-5d was taken by Rishton Angling Association, which charged one penny to enter its grounds. (That's 1661 pennies) Was it, or wasn't it? Rumour said that a well-known Rishton prankster was responsible for '*the sweet notes of the warbler*'.

The Leeds & Liverpool Canal. The Clayton-le-Moors to Blackburn section of the canal was opened in 1810. The photograph, taken from Tottleworth Bridge, shows a barge pulled by a horse before the 1939-45 war. The large mill on the left is the Victoria (Co-op) built 1861-3, and across the canal is the cotton storage warehouse (light roof) which was connected to the mill by a covered overhead passage. On the right is Britannia Mill built 1861-3 with later additions.

The canal agent's house on the north side of High Street next to the canal bridge is the oldest house in 'Rishton Town'. It was built by the Leeds & Liverpool Canal Co. about 1836 as a residence for their agent. In 1885 James Hindle Sutcliffe lived there and was Canal Bank Ranger. He was still there in 1909 before the family moved to Master Barn Farm.

BLACK AND WHITE PIERROTS.   RISHTON.

Much of the entertainment in the village was provided by members of churches. Each denomination had its own event, and concert parties were popular. The Pierrots performed in Harwood Road School before the 1914-18 war.

St. Peter and St. Paul Infant School. A class in 1905 when girls wore pinafores and boys wore collars - and most children wore clogs.

The Rishton Industrial Co-operative Society began when a few friends rented a shop in High Street for the sale of groceries. The society was registered in January 1864, and in 1865 moved to premises near the present Post Office. In 1866 it moved again to Edward Street and started to sell drapery and footwear.

By 1873 there were 250 members when land was obtained in Commercial Street and a store and two cottages were completed in 1874. The sale of furniture began in 1876, and the store was extended; the stone on the parapet was dated 1877. The Central premises were re-organised in 1907, when an Assembly Hall was added, and a new bakery replaced a smaller one in School Street.

Branch shops were opened in Cliff Street in 1910, St. Charles Road in 1914, a Boot and Shoe Department, now the 'Centre' opened in School Street in 1924, with an entrance in Commercial Street to the Cloggers, a busy place on Friday evenings when customers sat on forms awaiting their turn.

In 1951 the membership was 2,150. In 1967 Blackburn Co-operative took over the Society and the Central premises were demolished in 1972.

The photographs, taken in the 1930s, show Butcher's, Grocery, Ladies Outfitting, Confectioner's and Offices. The Butcher's at Christmas with Sidney Milner and Charles Garret, Manager. Every Christmas a temporary Toy Department was set up over the Outfitting Departments, more for 'Hope' than acquisition by most children.

Blackburn East Generating Station.
The first sod was cut in August 1919, and a concrete raft was laid as the ground was waterlogged. The official opening ceremony was performed by Lord Derby on 21st October 1921, when half the station was working. Coal could be delivered by canal, rail or road, and carried by overhead crane to bunkers which fed the boilers. Water was taken from the canal and after use pumped into wooden towers and cooled down to a temperature of about 75 degrees, to be reused or returned to the canal. Blackburn Corporation presented a Bill to Parliament to extend Blackburn's boundaries, in order to transfer an area of 193.674 acres on which the power station stood, from Rishton to Blackburn. Rishton Council submitted a petition against the Bill to the House of Commons during the 1922 Session, and the Bill was quashed.

Between 1942 and 1954 four concrete cooling towers were built. Production of electricity ceased in 1972 and in May 1983 the concrete towers were demolished.

Inauguration of

Blackburn East Generating Station

by

The Rt. Hon. The Earl of Derby, K.G., P.C., G.C.V.O., C.B.

Mayor - Joseph Fielding, J.P., Alderman.

Chairman of the Electricity Committee - Mr. Councillor H. Russell Hornby, J.P.

Town Clerk - Sir Lewis Beard.

Engineer - P. P. Wheelwright, Esq., M.I.E.E.

MENU.

Oxtail Soup.

Soles. Sauce Hollandaise.

Roast Beef.

Horseradish. Potatoes and French Beans.

Apple Tart and Cream.

Apricot Pudding and Wine Sauce.

Cheese. Biscuits. Celery.

Coffee.

TOAST LIST.

The King, The Duke of Lancaster.

The Mayor.

The Blackburn Electricity Undertaking and the Engineer.

James Meadowcroft, Esq., J.P.

Mr. Councillor H. Russell Hornby, J.P.

P. P. Wheelwright, Esq., M.I.E.E.

The Contractors.

Mr. Alderman Forrest, O.B.E.

Sir Charles Ellis, G.B.E., K.C.B.

The Rt. Hon. The Earl of Derby, K.G., P.C., G.C.V.O., C.B.

Lieut.-Commander P. T. Dean, V.C., M.P.

The Guests.

Sir Henry Norman, Bart., J.P.

The Rt. Hon. The Lord Mayor of Manchester.

The Mayor of Blackburn.

21st October, 1921.

Rishton Station, here captured on 20th June 1964 by local train buff Geoff Robinson. The 'Big 8' steam loco No. 48080 is seen returning empty coal wagons to the collieries in Burnley or West Yorkshire.

Rishton Station, and the Blackburn to Accrington section of the East Lancashire Railway was opened on 19th June 1848. Rishton's first station was a small wooden structure situated where Blackburn Road crosses the line. A station was erected on the present site in 1852, and a footbridge and booking office were built in 1893. The footbridge had a roof added in 1896, but this was removed after the Second World War.

Railway Station, Rishton

Rishton Motor Company was founded in 1920. The shareholders were Edgar Harrison, post master, who was Secretary; John Noble, builder; Bernard Smith, butcher; Joseph Bracewell, farmer; Thomas Carr, bBaker; James Lord, papermill managing director; and Herbert Wilson, foreman.

In 1923 the company amalgamated with Antley Bus Company and bought a sixth bus 'Star of the Road'.

Left is the Company's Office on the corner of High Street and Commercial Street.

Below is 'Star of the Road' outside the Post Office with driver Walter Carney.

RISHTON MOTOR CO. LTD.

PASSENGER SERVICE

Weekdays and Sundays.

BLACKBURN to RISHTON & CLAYTON	RISHTON (Roebuck) to CLAYTON	CLAYTON to HARWOOD	HARWOOD to RISHTON (Harwood rd)	RISHTON (Harwood rd) to BLACKB'N
	12-50 p.m.	1-0 p.m.	1-20 p.m.	1-30 p.m.
1-30 p.m.	1 50 ,,	2-0 ,,	2 20 ,,	2-30 ,,
2-30 ,,	2-50 ,,	3-0 ,,	3-20 ,,	3-30 ,,
3-30 ,,	3 50 ,,	4-0 ,,	4-20 ,,	4-30 ,,
4-30 ,,	4-50 ,,	5-0 ,,	5-20 ,,	5-30 ,,
5-30 ,,	5-50 ,,	6-0 ,,	6 20 ,,	6-30 ,,
6-30 ,,	6-50 ,,	7-0 ,,	7-20 ,,	7-30 ,,
7-30 ,,	7-50 ,,	8-0 ,,	8-20 ,,	8-30 ,,
8-30 ,,	8-50 ,,	9-0 ,,	9-20 ,,	9-30 ,,
9-30 ,,	9-50 ,,	10-0 ,,	10-10 ,,	10-20 ,,
10-30 ,,	10-50 ,,		11-0 ,,	

BLACKBURN to RISHTON & HARW'D	RISHTON (Harwood rd) to HARW'D	HARWOOD to CLAYTON	CLAYTON to RISHTON	RISHTON (Roebuck) to BLACK'B'N
	1-20 p.m.	1-30 p.m.	1 45 p.m.	1-0 p.m.
2 0 p.m.	2-20 ,,	2 30 ,,	2-45 ,,	2 0 ,,
3-0 ,,	3 20 ,,	3 30 ,,	3-45 ,,	3 0 ,,
4-0 ,,	4 20 ,,	4-30 ,,	4-45 ,,	4-0 ,,
5-0 ,,	5-20 ,,	5 30 ,,	5 45 ,,	5-0 ,,
6-0 ,,	6-20 ,,	6-30 ,,	6-45 ,,	6 0 ,,
7-0 ,,	7-20 ,,	7 30 ,,	7-45 ,,	7-0 ,,
8-0 ,,	8-20 ,,	8-30 ,,	8-45 ,,	8 0 ,,
9-0 ,,	9-20 ,,	10-35 ,,	9-45 ,,	9 0 ,,
10-10 ,,	10 25 ,,		10-50 ,,	10 0 ,,
10-35 ,,	10-50 ,,		11-0 ,,	

This Time Table is subject to revision without notice
TOURS TO ALL PARTS ARRANGED.
TAXI FOR HIRE.   Telephone : 66, Great Harwood.

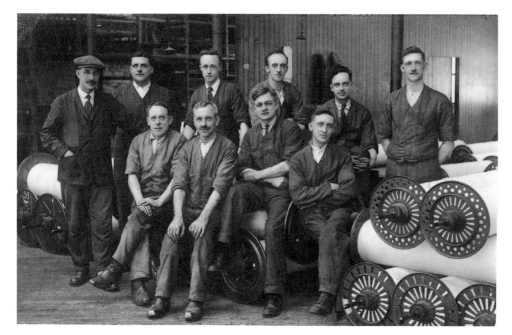

York Mill. The building was erected in 1910 by James Boardman and J. W. Baron, cotton manufacturers of Great Harwood. The first sod was cut in April and by September cotton cloth was being made, due to a bet by George Taylor of the York Mill Co., who leased the mill and ran the business. He asserted that he would be weaving within six months and to win the bet installed a loom run by a donkey engine!

Tacklers in the warehouse in the 1920s.

The machinery was powered by a double expansion cross-compound horizontal engine of 500HP made by Clayton and Goodfellow. The two cylinders were named 'Geoffrey' after the son of George Taylor, and 'Kathleen' after the daughter of Mr. Baron. The photograph shows E. Stoddart, engine tenter and Alfred Woods, the first manager.

R. H. Kenyon Ltd.

PLUMBING, HEATING

BUILDING CONTRACTORS

Hydraulic Rams Boiler Feed
Pumps a Speciality.
Frostproof Pipes and Valves
Domestic Sanitation.
Fire Ranges of all types
supplied and fixed.

◇

22, HIGH STREET, RISHTON

Telephone: GREAT HARWOOD 2094

Victoria Mill or **Co-op Mill** housed spinning frames as well as weaving looms. The mill closed in 1931.

Wellington Mill. Built in 1894-5 by Robert Clayton and worked by John Whittaker until 1908. Then the Wellington Mill Co. was formed, and in 1917 the Great Harwood Commercial Co. Ltd. purchased the mill and renamed it 'Unity'. There was little weaving after a fire in 1930, and in 1932 it was sold to John Grimshaw, timber merchant.

LOAD OF CABINS LEAVING WORKS.
JACK GRIMSHAW. UNITY APPLIANCE WORKS. RISHTON.
PHONE: 83 GT. HARWOOD.

45

The temporary **War Memorial** in November 1919. It was near to the lamp-post given by Mr. Thomas Steed to assist people walking from the station before Station Road was illuminated. The permanent Memorial on Blackburn Road is 22 feet high and made of Creetown granite, and was dedicated on 6th October 1923 by Mrs. E. Lewis, who had three sons killed during the war.

Rishton Papermill. Built on the site of an 18th century carding engine, powered by Spaw Brook, the Papermill commenced manufacture in 1874. It first produced newsprint and later art and chromo papers. Buildings included roadside offices, weigh house with weigh bridge dated 1919, former beam engine and turbine houses and brick chimney. The large ancillary works, built in 1904-6, on the south side of the road are visible on the right. Papermaking ended about 1980.

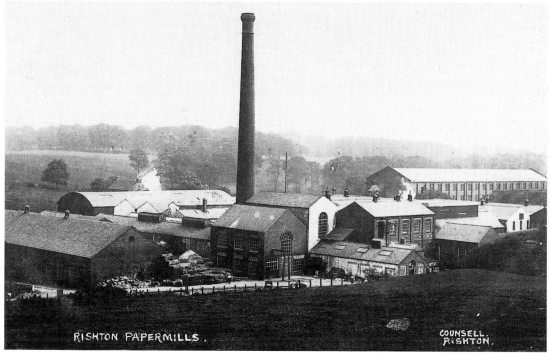

The Croft, Tottleworth. The larger cottage on the right side of the path has a datestone of 1758 and the initials of John and Jennet Fielden. John is described in the Parish Register as husbandman, and both he and Jennet are buried in the North Aisle of Great Harwood Church. This substantial cottage indicates prosperity in the mid-18th century. The smaller attached cottage predated John's as it had a datestone of 1746. Estate and Parish documents suggest that it was the home of Roger Fielden, shoemaker, a trade followed by several generations of this branch of the family. It was demolished and rebuilt in 1946.

THE SHOE STORE

*For all Your
Footwear
Requirements*

•

46, HIGH STREET, RISHTON

Old Ellen's, Tottleworth. Long before buses, the way to Great Harwood on foot was by Moor Lane and through Tottleworth, passing this cottage. Outside her door is Ellen Riding, born in 1831, who was a cotton warper, but as an old lady sold sweets from a table in her front room. In the 1930s elderly people could remember stopping there when young - if they had a halfpenny.

The cottage was reduced to a small heap of stones in the 1920s. The young gentleman is reported to be Tom Counsell - later the photographer.

Manor Farm, Tottleworth. the name does not refer to the Manor of Rishton, but to Great Harwood. It was owned by the Hesketh family of Rufford, who were joint Lords of the Manor of Great Harwood, and the large barn opposite the house was their Tithe Barn. In 1819 George Petre of Dunkenhalgh bought Manor Farm, several cottages and a great deal of land in Tottleworth from Sir Thomas Hesketh. The photograph, taken about 1900, shows that the windows on the left have been replaced by Georgian windows but the dripstone still remains. Unlike other houses of the period, Manor Farm had no porch.

A photograph taken during the 1926 General Strike when coal which had previously been discarded became valuable to men without a wage.

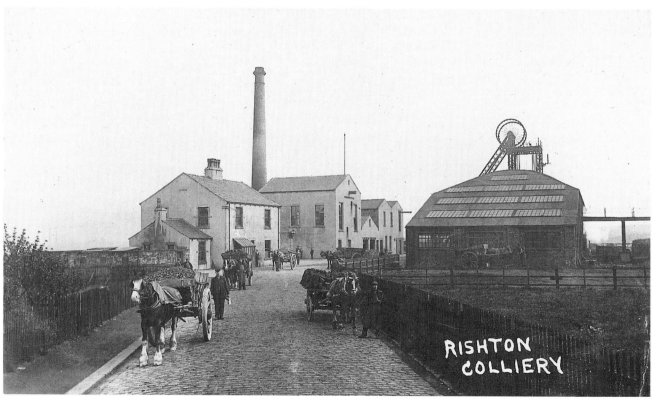

Rishton Colliery. Shafts were sunk at Meadowhead by Joseph Barnes and Co. about 1850, and cottages built there for employees.

Dunkenhalgh Colliery Co. was formed in 1874, and worked the pits until their exhaustion. The manager, Peter Wright Pickup, negotiated a lease in 1882-3 for an unworked coalfield further west. A new shaft was commenced at the end of Walmesley Street on 9th January, 1884, and finished on 8th July. Coal was found on Thursday 20th November, and two days later a dinner to celebrate was given by Mr. Pickup at the Walmesley Arms for colliers and their wives. A tramroad ran east from the workings to the canal, and a Yates and Thom (Blackburn) winding engine, and a generator by Fowler of Leeds were installed to work the colliery. In the 1930s, 230 colliers were employed. Operations ceased in 1941.

In 1960 the Coal Board demolished some of the buildings in order to instal two new pumps to pump water to Dean Reservoir. The only building then remaining was the Weigh Office. In 1984 William Smith of Oswaldtwistle, who worked at Rishton Pit from 1925 to 1941, recalled a painted board at the bottom of the shaft, which read '179 yards deep, 33 feet below sea level'. He said that the height of the coalface varied from 22 to 28 inches, and the haulage roads were around 36 inches in height.

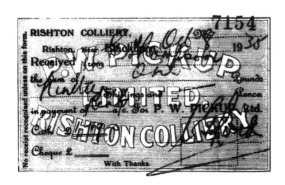

FALLING CHIMNEY RISHTON COLLIERY. NOV. 27TH 1913. COUNSELL RISHTON

George Tomlinson, the fourth son of John Wesley and Alice Tomlinson, was born at 55, Fielding Street, Rishton on 21st March, 1890. He attended the Weslyan School, and when 12 years old started working half-time as a weaver in a cotton mill. At 22 he was elected President of the Rishton Weavers' Association, and two years later became a councillor. On 4th September, 1914, he married Ethel Pursell, a mill worker, and the following year moved to Farnworth, travelling the town with a horse and cart selling herbal drinks made by his brother-in-law. From 1916 to 1919 he was an agricultural labourer. Returning to Farnworth after the war he became involved in local government there, being particularly interested in education, and was elected to Lancashire County Council in 1931. George returned to Rishton in 1937 when he was appointed Secretary of the Rishton Weavers' Association, and was soon County Councillor for Hyndburn. In 1938 he was elected M.P. for Farnworth, and from 1941-45 was Parliamentary Secretary to the Minister of Labour. In 1945-47 he was Minister of Works, responsible for much post-war building, and from 1947-51 Minister of Education. In addition to industrial and political interests, he was also a lay reader for over 40 years. George died on 22nd September, 1952, and was buried at Golders Green Cemetery, London.

Raising funds for servicemen during the 1914-18 war or a celebration after it had ended? The York Mill float in Danvers Street near the mill entrance.

The Free Gardeners' Club. During the years 1893-4 a Sick Club was formed by a group of Scots who worked at Rishton Papermill. The club met at the Roebuck, but a few years later premises were built on Parker Street, and extended in 1900. The club had a bowling green which was acquired by Rishton Urban District Council in 1950.
The photograph shows the Tug-of-War Team in 1912.

St. Peter & St. Paul's School. On 16th May, 1864, when Rishton had no church, the foundation stone of a new building was laid in Harwood Road. In 1866 this was licensed for Divine Worship and on 28th January, 1867, the Day School was opened. Designed by Taylor & Froggett, Architects of Blackburn, the contractors were Christopher Parker and Christopher Boardman of Rishton. Stone from the quarries was used, and much of the labour was voluntary. By 1870 there were less than 100 pupils, but with industrial development in the village numbers grew steadily, and more classrooms were added. School fees in 1881 were 4d per week. In 1883 the infants left when their new

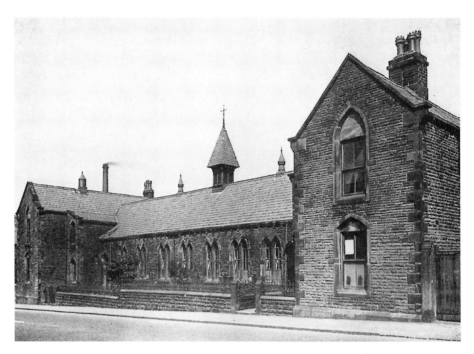

school in Commercial Street was built, and in 1886 thirty pupils were withdrawn when the Roman Catholic School opened at the Hermitage. In 1921 moveable glazed partitions were installed at Harwood Road, making eight separate classrooms. When the new school in Arundel Street opened on 4th March, 1961, Harwood Road was abandoned and was demolished in 1962.

On Saturday 27th January, 1940, it snowed and snowed. Sunday afternoon was punctuated by cracking sounds as troughings fell. Monday - still snowing, no buses. The road to Blackburn was completely blocked between the reservoir and Whitebirk.

To get to work it was necessary to plod through snow to the station and wait and wait. Perhaps a train might appear in an hour. The only comfort was a roaring fire in the waiting room. A week later when buses could get through to Blackburn, there was no view from the upper windows over the piled up snow.

Reginald Hargreaves of 16, Albert Street was a Mineral Water Manufacturer in 1915. Is this him, standing beside his Model-T Ford sometime after the 1914-18 war?

GEORGE PENSON
F. PENSON

Decorator

High-Grade Workmanship
Reasonable Prices

Agent for:—
CROWN WALLPAPERS · BROLAC ENAMEL
PAINT · BRISTOL HARD GLOSS PAINT

14, HIGH STREET, RISHTON
Telephone: 2080

Rishton Mill was the first weaving shed in Rishton. It was erected by the side of the canal in 1851, and closed in 1930. The photograph taken in 1911, at the time of the Coronation, shows Fred Spencer, Naomi Hanson and Mrs. Fred Spencer standing before a decorated tackler's bench in the weaving shed.

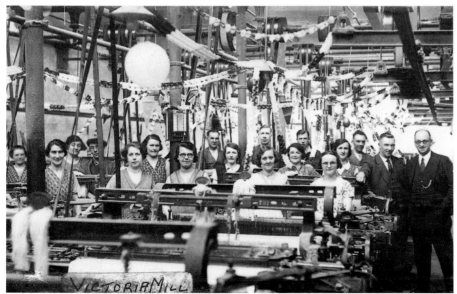

During the Coronation of 1937 there were six mills still weaving cotton. All were decorated for the Coronation.

The Local Board was formed on 23ʳᵈ June, 1882. When Boards were abolished it became an Urban District Council, and held its first meeting on 31ˢᵗ December, 1894. It met in a rented cottage, 68, High Street, described by a Councillor in 1896 as '*a badly adapted cottage, the council chamber a back kitchen, even to fire grate, oven and boiler*'. By 1899 the office was in a rented house 4, Church View. Land was purchased in Brook Street, and after several years building began. The new office and fire station, which cost about £2,200, was built to the plan of Mr. J. Cornall, the surveyor. It was brick with stone facings, and contained on the ground floor an enquiry office, overseer's and collector's office and two storerooms. On the first floor were the clerk's office, surveyor's office with drawing tables, and a Council Chamber 28 feet by 18 feet with an oak table to accomodate twelve members and officials. On 30ᵗʰ June, 1909, the Council Office was formally opened by the Chairman, Mr. Bernard Smith. Due to the formation of Hyndburn District in 1974, the Brook Street office was disused and was demolished in 1991. This photograph was taken outside the Council Offices, which also housed the Fire Brigade, in 1910.

Fire! Fire! April 1895 the Urban District Council place a box near the Roebuck. It contained a stand pipe and a length of hose. Fourteen men are engaged at 10s per annum to act as a Fire Brigade. October 1896, Sunday 2.0am. Fire at Bridgefield Mill - no bell to summon the Brigade so fire well alight when Brigade arrives. Consternation! Difficulty in getting water from hydrants at back Spring Street. Solution - run pipes through houses from main in street. Telephone Clayton, Blackburn and Great Harwood for assistance. Blackburn will not come. Clayton Steam Engine arrives 3.20am and pumps water from the canal. Accrington Brigade arrives soon after, followed by Great Harwood. By 4.0am fire under control, watched by audience of hundreds. Two winding frames and warping room destroyed and 40 to 50 people out of work until machinery replaced.

After this drama the Council order a Steam Engine from Merryweather & Sons. The engine, costing £375, can pump 450 gallons a minute. Permission is obtained to take water from the canal for testing and practice purposes. A shed for the engine is built on Council land in Cliff Street. When did the Council order an engine? Not until 1902.

The new Council Office building of 1909 incorporated a Fire Station at the west end, with stalls for four horses at the rear and a hay loft over. The station could accommodate two engines, but only housed one engine and a hose carriage.

In 1923 the Fire Brigade was disbanded and in 1929 the station became Rishton's first Public Library.

At the beginning of the Second World War the Auxiliary Fire Service used the Fire Station.

Class at Rishton C of E School, Summer 1934. The compiler of this book is fourth from the right on the second row. The pupils were, from the left:

Back row: Tom Wolstenholme, Wilf Sowerbutts, Ronald Robinson, Leonard Haslam, John Stoddart, Charlie Maclachlan, Leonard Sowerbutts, George Duckworth, Harry Dawson.

Third row: Elizabeth Luke, Enid Eddleston, Norma Nixon, May Greaves, Doris Cheetham, Norah Ingleson, Peggy Hacking, Brenda Smith, Bessie Clarkson, Elsie Almond.

Second row: Sid Pickup, William Wilkinson, Edna Procter, Ruby Benson, Lucy Harwood, Marjorie Passmore, Olga Connell, Kathleen Ormerod, Harry Crabtree, Kenneth Haworth, William Clarkson.

Front row: Jack Wolstenholme, Jack Bailey, Clifford Johnston, Jack Duckworth, Ronald Melling, William Sumner, Raymond Bond, Jack Sanderson.